Read-About® Geography

Iowa

By Reshma Sapre

Consultant
Donna Loughran
Reading Consultant

Children's Press®
A Division of Scholastic Inc.
New York Toronto London Auckland Sydney
Mexico City New Delhi Hong Kong
Danbury, Connecticut

Designer: Herman Adler Design
Photo Researcher: Caroline Anderson
The photo on the cover shows a farm in Crawford County, Iowa.

Library of Congress Cataloging-in-Publication Data

Sapre, Reshma.
  Iowa / by Reshma Sapre ; consultant, Donna Loughran.
    p. cm. — (Rookie read-about geography)
  Includes index.
  ISBN 0-516-22753-X (lib. bdg.)   0-516-25930-X (pbk.)
  1. Iowa—Juvenile literature. 2. Iowa—Geography—Juvenile literature.
  I. Loughran, Donna. II. Title. III. Series.
  F621.3.S27 2004
  917.77—dc22   \
                            ℭ ᐧ
                                        2004000469

CHILDREN'S PRESS, and ROOKIE READ-ABOUT®,
and associated logos are trademarks and or registered trademarks
of Scholastic Library Publishing. SCHOLASTIC and associated logos
are trademarks and or registered trademarks of Scholastic Inc.

1 2 3 4 5 6 7 8 9 10 R 13 12 11 10 09 08 07 06 05 04

Where does the tall corn grow?

It grows in Iowa (EYE-uh-wuh). Sometimes Iowa is called "The Corn State."

CANADA

WASHINGTON
OREGON
MONTANA
IDAHO
WYOMING
NEVADA
UTAH
CALIFORNIA
ARIZONA
NEW MEXICO
COLORADO
NORTH DAKOTA
SOUTH DAKOTA
NEBRASKA
KANSAS
OKLAHOMA
TEXAS
MINNESOTA
WISCONSIN
MICHIGAN
IOWA
ILLINOIS
MISSOURI
ARKANSAS
LOUISIANA
INDIANA
KENTUCKY
TENNESSEE
MISSISSIPPI
ALABAMA
OHIO
WEST VIRGINIA
VIRGINIA
NORTH CAROLINA
SOUTH CAROLINA
GEORGIA
FLORIDA
NEW HAMPSHIRE
VERMONT
MAINE
MASSACHUSETTS
NEW YORK
PENNSYLVANIA
RHODE ISLAND
CONNECTICUT
NEW JERSEY
DELAWARE
MARYLAND
Washington, D.C.

North
West   East
South

ALASKA   CANADA
MEXICO
HAWAII

5

Hog ranch

Farmers in Iowa grow
more corn than in any
other state.

They also grow soybeans
and oats. They raise hogs
and cattle, too.

Iowa is in the middle of the United States. It sits between two big rivers.

The Missouri River is to the west. The Mississippi River is to the east.

SOUTH DAKOTA

MINNESOTA

WISCONSIN

I O W A

⭐ Des Moines

Missouri River

Des Moines River

Mississippi River

NEBRASKA

MISSOURI

ILLINOIS

North
West ✦ East
South

SCALE 1 inch = 70 miles
0   Miles   70

0   Kilometers   110

9

Mississippi River

Low hills cover the south.
Lakes and swamps cover
the north.

Rocky hills and cliffs run
along the Mississippi River
on the east.

Wildflowers such as prairie lilies grow in the summer. Sunflowers bloom in the fall.

Sunflowers

American goldfinch

Birds nest on the farms in Iowa. The American goldfinch is the state bird.

Loon

Water birds live on Iowa's
lakes and rivers. A loon's
call sounds like someone
is laughing.

Pelicans scoop up fish
in their pouches.

Pelican

You can see different kinds of animals at the Iowa State Fair.

Blue ribbons go to the best cows, pigs, and sheep.

17

Many people visit the Iowa State Fair each year. Some enter contests. They call hogs and turkeys.

A man playing a harmonica

They play the harmonica
or banjo.

The State Fair is in Des Moines. Des Moines is the capital and largest city.

People who live here have many different jobs.

Des Moines

These people are going sledding.

After work, people in Iowa like to play.

The winters are cold and snowy. People ski, sled, and play hockey.

In the summer, it is hot.
People swim, fish, and hike.

Some travel down the
Mississippi River on
a riverboat.

Iowa has many special
places to visit, too.

There is a living history farm in Des Moines. Visitors learn how people lived in the 1800s.

There are lots of things
to do in Iowa.

What would you like
to do?

Words You Know

American goldfinch

Des Moines

hogs

living history farm

30

loon

Mississippi River

pelican

riverboat

31

Index

About the Author

Reshma Sapre is a freelance writer who has published three international travel books for children and has a background in teaching and curriculum development. As an Indian-born New Yorker, Reshma has spent many years traveling around America, absorbing its rich culture, history and geography.

Photo Credits

Photographs © 2004: A Perfect Exposure/Ty Smeads: 17; Bruce Coleman Inc./Windland Rice: 12; Corbis Images: 22, 25, 31 bottom right (Julie Habel), 18 (Bob Krist), 15, 31 bottom left (Joe McDonald); Dembinsky Photo Assoc./ George E. Stewart: 13, 30 top left; Peter Arnold Inc./Carl R. Sams II: 14, 31 top left; PictureQuest/Tim Barnwell: 19; Robertstock.com: 3 (H. Abernathy), 21, 30 top right (J. Blank); Superstock, Inc./Jack Affleck: 28; Tom Bean: 10, 26, 27, 30 bottom right, 31 top right; Tom Till Photography, Inc.: cover; Woodfin Camp & Associates/Robert Frerck: 6, 30 bottom left.
Maps by Bob Italiano